Helen Keller

by Jane Sutcliffe
illustrations by Elaine Verstraete

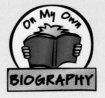

On My Own
BIOGRAPHY

Carolrhoda Books, Inc./Minneapolis

This book is available in two editions:
Library binding by Carolrhoda Books, Inc., a division of Lerner Publishing Group
Soft cover by First Avenue Editions, an imprint of Lerner Publishing Group
241 First Avenue North
Minneapolis, MN 55401 U.S.A.

Website address: www.lernerbooks.com

Library of Congress Cataloging-in-Publication Data

Sutcliffe, Jane.
    Helen Keller / by Jane Sutcliffe ; illustrations by Elaine Verstraete.
        p.   cm. — (On my own biography)
    Summary: Focuses on the early life of a woman who is well known for overcoming her handicaps of being both blind and deaf.
    ISBN: 0–87614–600–0 (lib. bdg. : alk. paper)
    ISBN: 0–87614–903–4 (pbk. : alk. paper)
    1. Keller, Helen, 1880–1968—Juvenile literature. 2. Blind-deaf women—United States—Biography—Juvenile literature. [1. Keller, Helen, 1880–1968. 2. Blind. 3. Deaf. 4. Physically handicapped. 5. Women—Biography.] I. Verstraete, Elaine, ill. II. Title. III. Series.
    HV1624.K4 S88 2002
    362.4'1'092—dc21   2001006585

Manufactured in the United States of America
2 3 4 5 6 7 – DP – 08 07 06 05 04 03

For my mother and my "Teacher," Clarice McCormick — J. S.

For my mother, always.
For Olivia and Megan. Thank you for your
imagination and dedication. — E. V.

Tuscumbia, Alabama
1886

Helen Keller reached out.

She touched warm, coarse hair.

Her busy fingers moved farther down.

They felt something smooth and wet.

Slap! A hairy tail smacked

into Helen's face.

Helen could not see
her family's milking cow.
But she liked touching it.
Helen Keller had been blind and deaf
for most of her life.
The only way she knew the world was by
touch, taste, and smell.

Helen was born in 1880
in Tuscumbia, Alabama.
When she was just a baby,
she became very sick.
The illness took away
her sight and hearing.
Helen could not hear her brothers'
laughter or her mother's voice.
She could not see her father's smile
or the pretty flowers outside her window.
For Helen, there was only silence
and gray darkness.

To learn to speak,

children need to hear words.

But Helen could not hear anything.

So she could not speak.

Instead, she made motions.

When she wanted her mother,

she put her hand against her face.

When she wanted her father,

she made the motion of putting on

a pair of glasses.

When she was hungry,

she pretended to slice and butter bread.

Helen knew she was different from
the rest of her family.
They moved their lips
when they wanted things.
Sometimes Helen stood between
two people as they talked.
She held her hands to their lips.
Then she tried moving her own lips.
But still no one understood her.

That made Helen angry.
Sometimes she screamed and cried
and kicked for hours.
She threw things and hit people.
But it didn't change anything.
She was still alone
in silence and darkness.

Helen was hard to control.

Her parents didn't know how to help her.

They took her to doctors.

None of the doctors could help Helen
see or hear again.

When Helen was six, a doctor suggested
the Kellers visit Alexander Graham Bell.

Dr. Bell was famous
for inventing the telephone.

He also taught deaf people.

Dr. Bell told the Kellers to write to
Michael Anagnos in Boston.
Mr. Anagnos was the head of
the Perkins Institution for the Blind.
He believed Helen could learn how
to let out the thoughts locked inside her.
Mr. Anagnos promised
to send Helen a teacher.

Helen and Teacher
March 1887

Helen's teacher came to live
with the Kellers that spring.
Her name was Annie Sullivan.
Annie had studied at the Perkins School.
She was nearly blind herself.
Annie needed to control Helen's wild
behavior so she could teach her.
But Helen did not understand
that Annie wanted to help her.
For two weeks, Helen fought with Annie.
She hit Annie and knocked out
one of her front teeth.
She even locked Annie in an upstairs room.
Mr. Keller had to get a ladder
and let Annie out through a window.

Still, Annie did not give up.

Little by little, Helen learned

to trust her new teacher.

Annie began to teach Helen about words.

She spelled words using her fingers.

Her hand formed a different shape

for each letter.

She pressed each shape

into Helen's hand.

When she gave Helen some cake,

she spelled C-A-K-E into Helen's palm.

When Helen held her doll,

Annie spelled D-O-L-L for Helen.

Helen imitated the shapes.

She thought it was a game.

She didn't know that the shapes

spelled words.

After a month, Helen could spell
whatever Annie spelled.
But Helen still did not know that she
was naming the things she touched.

One day Helen and Annie
walked to the well house.
Someone was pumping water.
Annie pushed Helen's hand
into the rushing water.
Helen felt the cool water on one hand.
She felt her teacher's fingers spelling
W-A-T-E-R into her other hand.
Over and over,
Annie spelled the word.
Suddenly Helen stood very still.
All at once she understood!
The liquid flowing over her hand
had a name.
It was W-A-T-E-R!

Everything had a name!

Helen wanted to learn them all.

She ran from one thing to another.

Annie spelled the name of everything

Helen touched.

Then Helen turned and pointed to Annie.

T-E-A-C-H-E-R, spelled Annie.

From then on, Helen's name for Annie

was "Teacher."

That summer, Helen learned

a lot of new words.

She stopped using her old motions.

Her fingers gave her

all the words she needed.

Annie did not teach Helen words
one at a time.
She talked to her in full sentences.
That way, Helen learned more
than just new words.
She learned new ideas.
Helen and Annie took long walks
through the woods and along the river.
Annie gave Helen lessons on the walks.
She showed Helen how seeds sprout
and plants grow.
She made mountains out of mud
and taught Helen about volcanoes.
Sometimes they climbed a tree
and had a lesson there.

Helen was hungry for knowledge.
She wanted to learn everything
Annie could teach her.
Soon Annie started teaching Helen
how to read.
The words were printed in raised letters
for a blind person.

Helen felt the words with her fingers.
She liked to hunt for words she knew.
When she learned to read better,
she read her books over and over.
Her curious fingers wore down
the raised letters.

Helen also learned to write.

She wrote letters to her family and Dr. Bell.

She wrote many letters
to Mr. Anagnos in Boston.

Mr. Anagnos was amazed by how much
Helen had learned.

He published some of Helen's letters.

Reporters began to write about Helen.

Soon she was famous.

People all over the world wanted to know
about the miracle girl.

And Helen wanted to know
all about the world.

Traveling
May 1888

Eight-year-old Helen sat on a train
with her teacher and her mother.
She was going to Boston to visit
the Perkins Institution for the Blind.
Helen wanted to hear all about
the countryside rushing past them.
Annie spelled into Helen's hand
everything she saw outside the window.
She described hills, rivers, forests,
and cotton fields.

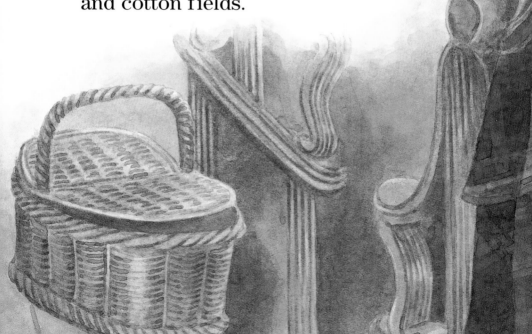

At the Perkins School,
Helen met Mr. Anagnos.
She also met children who knew
how to talk with their fingers.
"What joy to talk to other children in my
own language!" Helen wrote.
Helen also went to the ocean
for the first time.
She had only read about the ocean in books.
Right away, she ran into the water.
Then she tripped on a rock.
The water quickly closed over her head.
The waves tossed her back and forth.

It was as if they were playing
a game with her!
Finally she struggled toward the shore.
She was shivering and gasping for air.
She reached for her teacher's hand.
"Who put salt in the water?" she asked.
No one had told her that
ocean water was salty!

The world was opening up for Helen.
In three years she had learned
to finger spell, to read, and to write.
She even knew some French and Latin.
Everyone was astonished by how much
she had learned.
But Helen wanted to learn so much more.
She wanted to speak like other people.
She wanted to talk to her baby sister.
She wanted her dog to come
when she called.
She begged Annie to help her
find a way to speak.
When Helen was 10 years old,
Annie took her to a school in Boston.
A teacher there taught Helen to read lips
with her fingers.

Helen put her hand on a speaker's lips,
nose, and throat.
She learned to feel the words.
Then she tried to make her own sounds.
But her words never seemed
to come out quite right.

A few years later, Helen entered a school
for the deaf in New York City.
Helen loved New York.
She and Annie rode horses
in Central Park.

She went sledding
with the other students.
Once she climbed to the top
of the Statue of Liberty.

Helen also met many famous people.
When she met the writer Mark Twain,
they became friends at once.
His funny stories made her laugh
until she cried.
Still, one thing always made Helen sad.
She had worked day and night
to improve her speech.
But she had not learned to speak clearly.
Helen decided she would not let her
disappointment stop her from dreaming.

More to Learn

October 1896

At age 16, Helen was a young lady.

She was tall and strong.

She had a clever sense of humor.

She loved to swim and sail.

She could even row a boat herself.

She steered by the scent of the plants
that grew on shore.
Helen had always dreamed
of going to college.
To prepare, Helen entered
the Cambridge School for Young Ladies.

Up to now, Helen had gone to school
with other deaf or blind students.
At this new school, she lived with girls
who could see and hear.
She played games
and took long walks with them.
But everyone at her new school
had to speak to her through Annie.
They did not know how to finger spell.

Annie went to all of Helen's classes.

She spelled the lessons into Helen's hand.

Helen could not take notes

like the other students.

Her hands were "busy listening."

Helen studied hard.

After four years,

she was ready for college.

Helen entered Radcliffe College
in the fall of 1900.
She was the first deaf-blind person
ever to go to college.
As always, Helen wanted to learn
everything she could.
She took many classes.
Writing was her best subject.
She wrote about her first
dunking in the ocean.
She described how even she could see
the dazzle of sunlight on snow.
A magazine editor
heard about Helen's stories.
He knew that people would read them.
They wanted to know about the girl who
had broken out of her silent, gray world.

The editor asked Helen to write
about her life for his magazine.
Helen turned the stories into a book.
Her book was called *The Story of My Life.*
It was published in 1903.
Newspapers praised Helen's book.
Helen's friend Mark Twain wrote
with congratulations.
Helen had wanted so much
to speak to the world!
At last she had found a way.
Her book told the whole world
about her amazing life.

Helen Keller at about the age of 14

Afterword

Helen graduated from Radcliffe College in 1904. She spent the rest of her life helping the deaf and blind. Even though she never learned to speak as clearly as she wanted, she gave lectures to raise money for the American Foundation for the Blind. She wrote articles and books about her life and about her teacher.

Annie Sullivan stayed with Helen until Annie's death in 1936. The two of them had been together for nearly 50 years. A year later, Helen began touring the world on behalf of the blind. By the end of her life, she had traveled to 35 countries.

Helen had been famous almost all her life. From the time she was eight, she had met every president of the United States. She starred in two movies about her life. One of them, *The Unconquered*, won an Academy Award in 1955. A famous play, *The Miracle Worker*, was written about Helen and Annie.

Wherever Helen went, she charmed and amazed the crowds that came to see her. She reminded them that, with hard work, anyone can make a dream come true.

Important Dates

1880—Helen Adams Keller is born in Tuscumbia, Alabama, on June 27.

1881—Helen becomes deaf and blind after an illness.

1887—Annie Sullivan comes to Tuscumbia to teach Helen.

1894—Helen moves to New York City to attend school.

1896—Helen attends the Cambridge School for Young Ladies.

1900—Helen enters Radcliffe College.

1903—Helen's first book, *The Story of My Life*, is published.

1904—Helen graduates from Radcliffe College.

1924—Helen begins work for the American Foundation for the Blind.

1936—Annie Sullivan dies.

1964—Helen is awarded the Presidential Medal of Freedom by President Lyndon Johnson.

1968—Helen dies in Connecticut at age 87 on June 1.

1996—*The Story of My Life* is named one of the New York Public Library's Books of the Century.